Chemtastrophe!

D1460003

Chemistry Around the House

Erin Knight

Crabtree Publishing Company
www.crabtreebooks.com

Crabtree Publishing Company
www.crabtreebooks.com

Photographs: Title page: Laurence Gough/Shutterstock Inc.; p.2 : Wikimedia Commons; p. 3: Teacept/Shutterstock Inc.; p. 4: Evgeny Karandaev/Shutterstock Inc.; p. 5: Kaczor58/Shutterstock Inc.; p. 6: (top) Artiomp/Shutterstock Inc.; (bottom) 3DDock/Shutterstock Inc.; p. 7: (left) Ivan Bondarenko/ Shutterstock Inc., (right) R. Legosyn/Shutterstock Inc., (bottom) Wikimedia Commons; p. 8: (middle) Ross Aaron Everhard/Shutterstock Inc., (right) Lorraine Kourafas/Shutterstock Inc., (top) Marylooo/Shutterstock Inc.; p. 9: Frantisek Czanner/Shutterstock Inc.; p. 11: (inset) Blinow61/Shutterstock Inc., (background) Andre Blais/Shutterstock Inc.; p. 12: Tatiana Popova/Shutterstock Inc.; p. 13: Blueking/Shutterstock Inc.; p. 14: Bluerain/Shutterstock Inc.; p. 15: Prism68/Shutterstock Inc.; p. 16: (top) Olivier Le Queinec/Shutterstock Inc., (bottom) Wikimedia Commons; p. 17: (top) Art Proem/Shutterstock Inc., (bottom) XAOC/Shutterstock Inc.; p. 18: Mrloz/iStockPhoto.com; p. 19: Alexander Raths/Shutterstock Inc.; p. 20-23: Jim Chernishenko; p. 24: HultonArchive/iStockPhoto.com; p. 25: (top) MarcusVDT/Shutterstock Inc., (middle) Shell114/Shutterstock Inc., (bottom) Wikimedia Commons; p. 26: (middle) Bork/Shutterstock Inc., (bottom left) David Brimm/Shutterstock Inc., (top) Scott Cornell/Shutterstock Inc.; p. 27: (top) Shmel/Shutterstock Inc., (bottom) Wikimedia Commons; p. 28: Laurence Gough/Shutterstock Inc.; p. 29: (top left) Bmaki/Shutterstock Inc., (bottom) Grandpa/Shutterstock Inc., (top right) Marema/Shutterstock Inc.; p. 30-31: Teacept/Shutterstock Inc.

Publishing plan research and development:

Sean Charlebois, Reagan Miller
Crabtree Publishing Company

Developed and Produced by: Plan B Book Packagers

Editorial director: Ellen Rodger

Art director: Rosie Gowsell-Pattison

Glossary and index: Nina Butz

Project coordinator: Kathy Middleton

Editor: Adrianna Morganelli

Proofreader: Molly Aloian

Prepress technician and production coordinator:

Margaret Amy Salter

Print coordinator: Katherine Berti

Special thanks to experimenter Natasha

"How we know" boxes feature an image of 19th century Russian scientist Dmitri Mendeleev who developed the first periodic table of elements, the basis for the modern table still used by scientists.

Library and Archives Canada Cataloguing in Publication

Knight, Erin, 1980-
     Chemistry around the house / Erin Knight.

(Chemtastrophe!)
Includes index.
Issued also in electronic format.
ISBN 978-0-7787-5283-7 (bound).--ISBN 978-0-7787-5300-1 (pbk.)

     1. Chemistry--Juvenile literature.
2. Chemistry--Experiments--Juvenile literature.
I. Title. II. Series: Chemtastrophe!

QD35.K55 2011   j540   C2010-906578-6

Library of Congress Cataloging-in-Publication Data

Knight, Erin.
 Chemistry around the house / Erin Knight.
     p. cm. -- (Chemtastrophe!)
 Includes index.
 ISBN 978-0-7787-5300-1 (pbk. : alk. paper) -- ISBN 978-0-7787-5283-7
(reinforced library binding : alk. paper) -- ISBN 978-1-4271-9608-8
(electronic (pdf))
 1. Chemistry--Experiments--Juvenile literature. I. Title.
QD38.K55 2011
540.78--dc22

                                              2010042061

Crabtree Publishing Company

www.crabtreebooks.com   1-800-387-7650

Printed in China/012011/GW20101014

Copyright © **2011 CRABTREE PUBLISHING COMPANY**. All rights reserved. No part of this publication may be reproduced, stored in a retrieval system or be transmitted in any form or by any means, electronic, mechanical, photocopying, recording, or otherwise, without the prior written permission of Crabtree Publishing Company. In Canada: We acknowledge the financial support of the Government of Canada through the Book Publishing Industry Development Program (BPIDP) for our publishing activities.

Published in Canada
Crabtree Publishing
616 Welland Ave.
St. Catharines, ON
L2M 5V6

Published in the United States
Crabtree Publishing
PMB 59051
350 Fifth Avenue, 59th Floor
New York, New York 10118

Published in the United Kingdom
Crabtree Publishing
Maritime House
Basin Road North, Hove
BN41 1WR

Published in Australia
Crabtree Publishing
386 Mt. Alexander Rd.
Ascot Vale (Melbourne)
VIC 3032

Contents

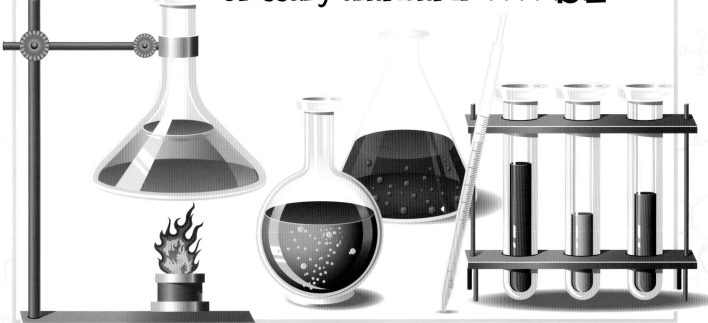

Lucky Science Accidents

What do you, a detective, and a scientist have in common? You all have questions about the world around you. You want to know why things happen.

So Many Questions

How do we find answers to our most baffling questions? Detectives study the evidence at the scene of a crime and use these observations to determine who committed the crime. Scientists carefully observe their surroundings and conduct experiments to understand how the world works. You pay attention to what you see on your way home from school, and without even realizing it, you might make your own hypothesis, or educated guess, about why it happened.

Science in Action

You do not need to be in a laboratory to see science in action. In fact, just about everything you find in your own home—the shampoo in the bathroom, the pizza in the oven, the gasoline in your parents' car—depends on chemistry. Chemistry is the branch of science concerned with **matter**. It deals with the substances that make up the world and looks at how these substances change and **react** together. For example, maybe you have noticed that ice cubes crack when you drop them into a glass of soda. Why? On a hot day, droplets of water will collect on the outside of the cold glass. How do they get there? This question and many more can be answered with a little bit of knowledge about the science of matter.

Water condenses on the outside of a soda glass.

Scientific Surprises

Scientists are careful thinkers and even better observers. They closely watch the world around them, and then they conduct experiments based on their observations to answer their questions about how matter works. Even with all of this thought and planning, many scientific discoveries take us by surprise. In fact, some of the most important scientific advances have been made by accident.

Careful Observation

One of the most famous scientific surprises changed the way doctors treat infections. Have you ever taken out a slice of bread and found it to be covered in fuzzy blue-green mold? Well, then you have something in common with Alexander Fleming, a Scottish **biologist** who was researching the **influenza virus**. The window in his laboratory was left open one day, allowing **mold spores** to enter and **contaminate** his experiment. Except…it turned out that his experiment was not ruined after all. He noticed that **bacteria** in his dishes would not grow where the mold spores had landed. He used this observation to develop penicillin, a medicine that has saved countless lives.

Clever observation of mold in a laboratory led to the discovery of penicillin—a happy accident of science.

Some scientific surprises save lives. Some just make a good breakfast. Breakfast cereal was invented when the Kellogg brothers decided to bake a batch of mushy wheat dough left on the stove for too long.

Matter Really Matters

Matter is anything that has mass and takes up space. Usually it is something that you can see or touch, like a soccer ball, a jar of mustard, or even a dog, but matter can take different forms including liquids and gases.

Atoms and Elements

All matter is made up of atoms. Atoms are particles so small that they cannot be broken down by any chemical process. Some things are only made up of one kind of atom. These are pure **substances**, called **elements**. Some common elements are gold, silver, oxygen, and iron. All known elements are listed in a chart called the periodic table. At the center of every atom is a nucleus. Surrounding the nucleus like a cluster of buzzing flies are sub-atomic particles called electrons and protons. These tiny, electrically charged particles help the atom make bonds with other atoms to become a molecule.

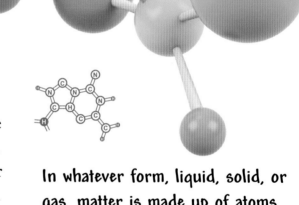

In whatever form, liquid, solid, or gas, matter is made up of atoms and molecules.

Molecules and Bonds

Molecules are made up of two or more atoms. Water, for example, is made up of two hydrogen atoms and one oxygen atom. Water's makeup, with two different kinds of atoms, can also be called a **compound**. Water is sometimes referred to by its chemical formula H_2O, with H standing for hydrogen and O standing for oxygen. These atoms are linked together by a chemical bond.

6

The Science of Mixtures

You might notice many mixtures around your home. In a mixture, such as soil and sand or tea and sugar, the particles mix together but do not form chemical bonds. They can be separated more easily than a compound. A common method of separating a mixture is **filtration**. You can improve the taste of the water that comes from your tap by pouring it through a **carbon** filter. The filter will remove some of the **impurities**.

Hot or cold tea is a mixture. Water poured through a filter has impurities removed, or separated.

HOW WE KNOW

Small But Mighty

Atoms are so small we cannot even see them with a regular microscope, so how do we know what they are made of, or if they even exist? We know by seeing the effect that they have on other things that we can measure.

Unless you look very closely, sugar and salt have similar appearances. Taste them and you will notice how their atoms and molecules differ.

Does Matter Matter?

Why are scientists concerned with molecules and atoms? Why should you be? The actions of atoms and molecules can explain why matter looks the way it does, why it acts the way it does, and why it might change from one form to another. The atoms and molecules that make up matter all have their own characteristics—qualities that make them different from other types of atoms or molecules. If we know what these qualities are, we can design tests to determine what something is made from. You may have done this yourself. A jar of sugar and a jar of salt might look exactly the same, but all it takes is a little taste and you will know immediately if you have the right ingredient to make lemonade!

fun fact

Alfred van Leeuwenhoek, a Dutch scientist who improved the microscope, first thought of magnifying pepper grains so that he could "discover the cause of the hotness or power whereby pepper affects the tongue."

Properties

The science of chemistry is often concerned with labeling and categorizing substances, which is like putting socks and T-shirts away in their proper drawers. One of the methods that scientists use to categorize matter is to observe its properties. Physical properties are things that you can see and describe such as matter's appearance, texture, color, and odor. Matter can be solid, liquid, or gas. It can also transform from one state to another. Ice for example, changes from a solid state to a liquid state (water) when it melts. This is called a physical change. This change takes place when temperature affects the speed at which molecules move around, and how tightly the molecules are bonded to one another. The molecules in frozen water move slower than the molecules in room temperature or boiling water —but they are still the same molecules.

Chemical Changes

The change of state from ice to water is easily reversed. This makes it a physical change. Some changes involve an interaction between the molecules that cause new material to be formed. Imagine you have left your bicycle out in the rain. After a few days, you may notice that rust appears on the chain. The rust was produced when the oxygen in the air reacted with the iron in your bicycle chain, forming iron oxide (the chemical term for rust). The rust will have the same mass as the original elements involved.

Leaves undergo a chemical change in the fall when they change color.

Scientific Method

Just like you, scientists are always asking questions. If they do not know the answer to a question, they pay careful attention to their observations and propose an explanation based on what they have seen.

Ask a Question, Pose an Answer

This proposed explanation is called a hypothesis. The word hypothesis comes from the ancient Greek word *hupothesis*, which roughly means "foundation." Scientists need a foundation to guide their investigations, so they begin with a question, give a proposed explanation or hypothesis, and then design an experiment to test their hypothesis. By following this process, they are using the scientific method. The scientific method takes "I wonder why" one step further. It is like thinking with a plan.

Scientific Method Steps

1. Ask a specific question.
   What causes a cake to rise when it is baked?

2. Gather information by observing, researching, and taking notes.
   Mixing different substances together can cause a physical or chemical reaction. The cake requires a list of specific ingredients.

3. Make a hypothesis.
   I hypothesize that one of these ingredients causes the cake to rise.

4. Design an experiment to test your hypothesis.
   I will make small batches of batter, each one leaving out a different ingredient. I will see if each cake will still rise.

5. Take careful notes and watch to see if your hypothesis is correct.
   When I left out the baking powder, the cake did not rise.

6. Tell others about your findings.

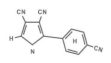

Whose Idea Was It, Anyway?

No one really knows who first identified the scientific method as a way of answering a complicated question. Ancient Greek mathematician Archimedes is often given the credit. When Archimedes was presented with a problem he didn't understand, he would think it through carefully. Then he would conduct practical experiments to see if his ideas were correct. Archimedes is famous for a lucky accident that helped him discover **displacement** while soaking in a tub. He noticed that when he immersed his body in the water, the water level rose, and when he stood up, the water level dipped.

fun fact

When talking about the experiments that led to his discovery of penicillin, Alexander Fleming was known to say, "I have been wonderfully lucky."

Everyday Chemistry

Chemistry is an exciting branch of science because you can apply what you know about it to everyday life, from the time you wake up until you go to bed.

A Day in Your Chemistry Life

Chemistry is everywhere. In your body, in your house, and in your neighborhood. Just think about your average morning. When you wake up in the morning, one of two things will happen. Chemicals in your brain will give your body the signal to wake up, or your alarm clock, powered by a chemical reaction that creates electricity, will ring and wake you with a start. Either way, chemistry gets the day going.

Turn on the Lights!

Maybe you yawn, and, if you are awake really early, you turn on the light. What causes the light to brighten? If you guessed that it has to do with chemistry, you have the right idea. Electrochemistry is the branch of chemistry that explains how electricity works.

Everything about this lamp can relate to the science of chemistry, from the materials to the electricity that powers it.

fun fact

Neurochemistry is the study of the chemical properties of the brain. It is a relatively new branch of chemistry that attempts to explain how the brain works.

Biochemistry for Breakfast

Chemistry is involved in the production of electricity, and also in the workings of your body. Biochemistry is the chemistry that occurs within every living thing. It always involves the element carbon, the fourth most abundant element on Earth. Digestion, respiration (breathing), and photosynthesis in plants are all examples of biochemical reactions.

When you head down for breakfast in the morning, you may hear your stomach growling. The air in your stomach is shifting around. When you think of the pancakes or cereal you are about to have, you may feel yourself **salivating**. The chemistry of your saliva will send a signal to your stomach that says you are about to eat, and it had better get ready. There are **enzymes** within your saliva and your stomach that will help to break down your breakfast. Your body will convert the **carbohydrates** in your breakfast into glucose—a sugar that your body uses for energy. When you breathe, glucose reacts with oxygen to release energy that is then used to pump your heart and move your muscles. All throughout the day, your body will be performing the chemical reactions that are essential to life.

Biochemistry is a branch of science that deals with chemical changes in living things. Eating breakfast creates a biochemical reaction in your body.

Around the House

The way the particles that make up solids, liquids, and gases are organized affects the way that matter behaves and what happens to it when it comes into contact with other substances.

Reactions In Your Environment

A chemical reaction takes place when two substances mix together and change each other's molecular structure by trading "partners." The bonds between their molecules might break apart, or new bonds might be made, leading to the formation of different molecules. These reactions can explain virtually everything that goes on around your home!

Chemistry Picks up the Pieces

Temperature affects the molecular structure of a substance. If heat is added, this energy breaks the bonds between molecules. In hot conditions, there is more space between each molecule, and the substance becomes more **pliable**. If you drop a glass onto the kitchen floor, it will smash to pieces. You would not be able to stick these pieces back together, or bend the pieces into different shapes. However, under the right conditions, glass is like modeling clay. When it is made, it is placed into an oven, called a kiln, that heats it to the point where the bonds between the molecules are loose enough that the glass becomes a liquid and can be molded.

A glassblower heats and molds glass into a form. It is then cooled to become solid.

Is it Hot, or Is it Just Me?

Different substances are affected by heat to different degrees. If an object is made of a material that conducts heat well, then heat energy will be conducted from one molecule to the next very quickly. If you stir a hot pot of soup with a metal spoon, you will not be able to hold the end of that spoon for very long. In contrast, you could leave a wooden spoon in the boiling soup for hours, and the end of the wooden spoon would still be cool to the touch. Metal conducts heat. Wood does not.

Insulation prevents hot or cold air from escaping a house—an example of how chemistry deals with materials and processes.

We use this principle in the building of our houses. In North America, the temperature outside can vary widely. Whether it is blazing hot outside or freezing cold, we want the temperature inside our houses to be comfortable for us. People use different kinds of energy to heat their houses in winter and cool their houses in summer, but none of these are very effective if the building is not insulated to prevent the hot or cool air from escaping. Most products that are used for insulation are synthetic, such as fiberglass or polystyrene. The spaces between the particles in these materials fill with air, preventing heat exchange.

15

fun fact

The Eiffel Tower in Paris, France, is almost six inches (15 cm) taller on the hottest day of summer than it is on the coldest day of winter. How can chemistry explain this mystery?

Chemistry of Cool

If you go out for a picnic or to a baseball tournament, you may keep your food from spoiling by carrying it in a cooler. The cooler will be made of a material that has insulating properties, and if you put an ice pack inside, it will keep things cold—for a while. Up until the 1920s, most households depended on an ice box to store food. Iceboxes kept things cold with ice. In fancy terms, this is called thermal insulation. The modern refrigerator makes use of both thermal insulation and a chemical reaction to cool food.

Modern refrigeration is a marvel of chemistry: using a chemical reaction to keep something cool.

HOW WE KNOW

The Invention of Fridges

William Cullen, a Scottish physician, thought a lot about the human body. Our bodies keep cool by producing sweat, which is mostly water. When the water on our skin **evaporates**, heat is absorbed, because evaporation requires heat energy to break bonds between the molecules so they can form a gas. Could this principle be applied to other objects? Dr. Cullen experimented with different liquids. He found that when a liquid called nitrous ether is evaporated, so much heat is absorbed by the reaction that freezing temperatures result. He pumped this liquid through a series of pipes, inventing the first refrigerator! It took a long time and much tweaking before refrigerators became a common sight in North American homes.

Non-Stick Pans

As our understanding of chemistry has grown, scientists have been able to create a number of products that do not exist in nature for us to use in our daily lives. Non-stick pans are common in most kitchens today and that's all because of a chemist's chemtastrophes, or failed experiments. In 1938, Roy Plunkett was trying to develop a non-toxic refrigerator coolant. One of his combinations of ingredients unexpectedly produced a strange white powder. After doing tests, he found that the powder was not affected by extreme temperatures, did not conduct electricity, and did not stick to anything. He called this surprising new compound Teflon. The product has many uses, from insulation for electrical wiring to making durable material for spacesuits.

Teflon, a coating used in non-stick cooking pans, was discovered by accident.

Preventing Stains By Accident

Another useful compound that does not exist in nature was discovered by the chemist Patsy Sherman. She was trying to develop a special type of rubber that could be used in the aviation industry when some of the compound spilled on her canvas tennis shoe. That part of the shoe stayed clean, even after a long, messy day in the laboratory, because the molecules within the compound do not easily combine with water or oil. She went on to use this technology to develop Scotchgard, a common stain-repellant used in clothing and furniture.

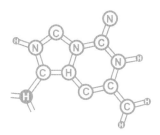

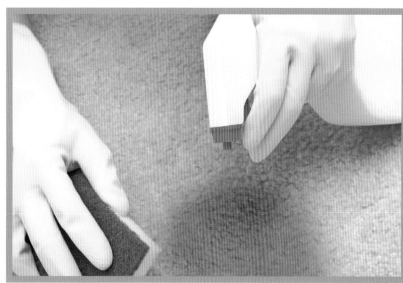

Scotchgard is now used on carpets to make them repel stains so they are easier to clean.

Testing 1-2-3

Most experiments are conducted because there is a problem to be solved. Even if the solution that is found is not always the one that scientists expect, experiments are always conducted with a specific question or problem in mind.

Ask a Question

Start an experiment by asking a question about an observation you have made. Gather as much information as you can, and propose a hypothesis that can be tested. For example, you may have observed that a pot of simmering hot water will come to a boil if you add salt. How does salt affect the boiling and freezing points of water?

Testing Method

To determine the effect of salt on the melting of ice, you could set four ice cubes on a tray. One would be your control, to which you would add nothing. In a science experiment, a control is the specimen that is not manipulated at all. On another ice cube, you could put one teaspoon of salt. On a third, you might put one teaspoon of sugar, and on a fourth, you could add a teaspoon of sand. The cubes with salt, sugar, and sand added are your variables. Variables are traits or conditions that can change during an experiment, but you should only manipulate one variable at a time. Here, all of the ice cubes must be the same size, and you must add the same amount of salt, sugar, or sand to each cube. If you are off on your measurements for each variable, or if you manipulate several variables at once, you will not know which change was responsible for the results.

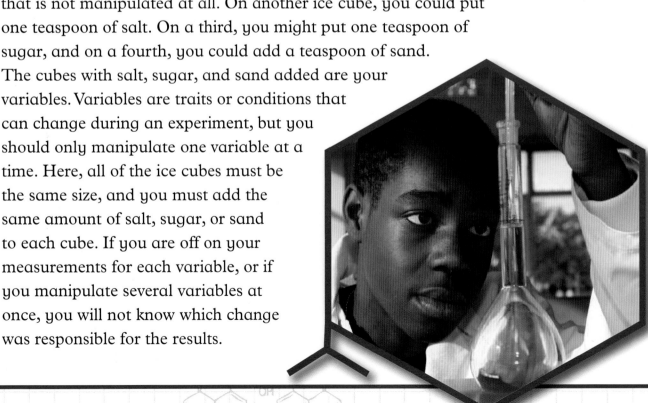

Careful Observation

Observation is the key to any scientific discovery. Throughout your experiment, you must pay close attention to the results and take careful note of what you see. These observations may become important later. You may observe that the ice cube with the salt begins to melt wherever the salt makes contact with the ice, but the other cubes melt from the corners first.

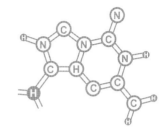

Analysis and Conclusion

Once you have carried out your experiment and have recorded your results, you can begin to analyze the results. Your experiment melting the ice cube will reveal that adding salt to ice will cause the ice to melt at a faster rate. Based on what you know about chemistry, the salt molecules must be reacting with the water molecules. Saltwater will remain a liquid at a lower temperature than pure water. When you analyze the results of your experiment, you will be able to come to a conclusion about why something happens, and apply this new knowledge to other situations.

A hypothesis cannot be proven until the experiment has been conducted many times. If the same results are achieved over and over again, the hypothesis can be called a theory.

Shiny as a New Penny

Have you ever wondered why pennies are so shiny and bright when they are new and how they get so dirty and dull?

Question: Can a dirty penny be made to look new?

Hypothesis: Cleaning pennies requires a reaction from a solution that is acidic.

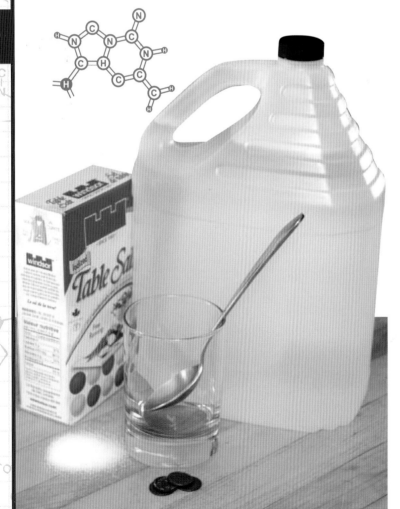

Materials:

1 cup (237 ml) of vinegar
¼ cup (75 grams) of salt
bowl
spoon
dirty pennies
paper towel

Method:

1. Pour vinegar and salt into the bowl and stir well.
2. Drop the pennies into the bowl and observe them closely.
3. Record your observations. When the pennies no longer look tarnished, remove them from the bowl and place them on the paper towel.

Pour the vinegar into the container, or glass, of salt.

Mix the vinegar and salt with the spoon.

Add the dirty pennies to the mixture.

Wait a few minutes, observe the changes, and remove the pennies when they look clean.

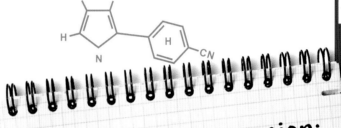

Results and Discussion:

A chemical reaction occurs between the vinegar (an acid) and the tarnish on the penny, which has formed as a result of the copper in the penny being exposed to the oxygen in air. The salt acts as a **catalyst**, which speeds up the reaction.

Is the penny as good as new? Come back and look at it a few hours later. What has happened? Can you hypothesize why it happened?

Cleaning Windows

Do you need a mass-made commercial cleaner from a store to make windows sparkle?

Question: What makes an effective window cleaner?

Hypothesis: Cleaning windows requires more than just water and soap.

Materials:

1/4 cup (59 ml) of white vinegar
1/2 teaspoon (2 ml) of dish soap
2 cups (473 ml) of water
spray bottle
cloth or rag

Procedure:

1. Pour vinegar, dish soap, and water into a spray bottle.
2. Mix.
3. Spray mixture on dirty glass or windows and wipe clean.
3. Record your observations.

Measure out the ingredients and fill a spray bottle. Shake to mix.

Spray a dirty window with the window cleaner mixture and wipe clean.

You can try cleaning a window with just water or with a commercially prepared window cleaner. Observe and record any differences in how clean the window gets.

Results and Discussion:

Vinegar is an acetic acid, which is mildly corrosive. It breaks down grease, mineral deposits, and soap buildup.

When mixed in a solution with water and a surfactant cleaner such as dish soap, vinegar acts as a mild cleaner capable of removing dirt and grime without streaking.

Try cleaning your window first with just water or the water/detergent mixture. How does the vinegar cleaner stack up?

Eureka! I Found It!

Have you ever had a moment where you have suddenly understood something, or where you have found a solution to a problem you have been working on? Some people call those times "eureka moments."

Archimedes was clever and observed the world around him.

I Have Found It!

The word "eureka" comes from the ancient Greek "heureka," for "found." Ancient scientist Archimedes is credited with using it as a cry of satisfaction after discovering a method for determining the purity of gold. Archimedes observed that water rose when he lowered his body into a bath. This gave him the idea that he could test the purity of the king's gold crown by measuring the amount of water it displaced. It was such a brilliant idea, and it came to him so quickly, that he jumped out of the tub and ran naked through the streets, shouting "Eureka!" or "I have found it!"

While no one knows if this story is actually true, many modern scientists have experienced their own eureka moments, stumbling across a fascinating idea that changed their understanding of the world.

fun fact

Glue used to be made from the byproducts of plants, fish, and animals, but most glues are now made from synthetic products.

The "Pop" of a Great Idea

Pop…pop…pop-pop-pop… If you are a fan of microwave popcorn, you might think that the microwave was designed with this delicious treat in mind. The American engineer Percy LeBaron Spenser probably had a grander plan when he started experimenting with **radar** in 1946. One afternoon after working on the project, he put his hand in his jacket pocket and realized that the candy bar he had been saving for a snack had melted.

He wondered if the magnetron that he had been using to produce radio waves had the power to heat food. What did he use to test his theory? Kernels of popping corn! Next, he directed the radio waves toward a raw egg in its shell. When it exploded in his colleague's face, he knew he was onto something important. Today's microwaves cause the molecules in food to vibrate 25 billion times a second, cooking the product much faster than traditional methods.

Microwave popcorn and Velcro shoe fasteners are two products that came about by accident.

HOW WE KNOW

Velcro: Observation + Science

Scientists often get the idea for a new material by observing similar structures that exist in nature. Georges de Mestral, a Swiss engineer, noticed that his dog would come home covered in burrs from the bush. When he looked at these burrs closely, he saw that they were made up of tiny hooks. He used these observations to develop Velcro.

Post-it Notes

A lot of busy families use sticky-notes to remind each other to buy milk, let the dog out, or go to the dentist. These simple time savers were invented by a chemist with the help of a failed experiment of another chemist! At adhesive manufacturing company 3M, chemist Spencer Silver developed a glue that was not very sticky. Arthur Fry, another chemist at 3M, was frustrated that the bookmarks he used for choir practice always fell out of his hymnbook. Fry decided to try using Silver's glue on paper to create a sticky note that wasn't too sticky. The first Post-it note was created! The first Post-it notes went on sale in 1980 and have been popular ever since.

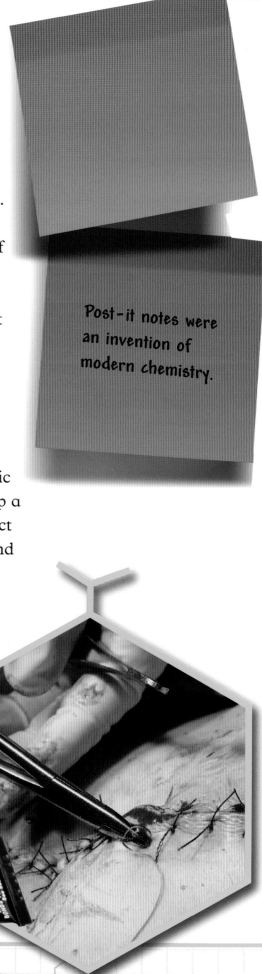

Post-it notes were an invention of modern chemistry.

Glued to Their Work

One of the strongest household glues—Super Glue, was also the result of a failed experiment. While working at Eastman Kodak, a company that produces photographic materials, Dr. Harry Coover had been hoping to develop a strong plastic that could be used in jet canopies to protect pilots. The compound was spread over a work surface and Coover found that the **prisms** he had been using were glued together—so he stuck with his idea. Coover had discovered cyanoacrylates, a group of chemicals that were strong adhesives. Cyanoacrylates such as Super Glue were used during the Vietnam War to patch injuries until surgery could be done. Today, they are still used in hospitals to glue instead of stitching skin.

Super Glue can glue skin together, which can be a miracle or a chemtastrophe!

No Rubber-Necking

Sometimes, chemistry is trial and error. Charles Goodyear was an unemployed salesman in 1839. He had been trying for years to find a way to make rubber, a natural product made from the gum of the rubber tree, more hard wearing. Natural rubber is very brittle in cold temperatures and becomes a sticky mess in the heat. Goodyear's first break came when he was stirring a mixture of sulfur, white lead, and rubber gum. When a few drops of the mixture spilled and hit the stove, he expected it would melt. Instead, the rubber only sizzled and became black and tough around the edges. It took him five more years before he was able to create the exact recipe for weatherproof rubber. The process used to weatherproof rubber is called vulcanization, named for Vulcan, the Roman god of fire.

Goodyear's experiments paved the way for synthetic vulcanized rubber used in many things including automobile and bike tires.

HOW WE KNOW

Environmental Chemtastrophes

Many everyday product manufacturers and chemical companies have dodgy environmental records. Some accidentally dump chemicals in waterways, or pollute the air during their manufacturing processes. Others have used materials labelled as persistent organic pollutants or POPs. POPs do not degrade or decompose in the environment, can be found in water, food, and air, and are harmful to the health of humans and animals. Many manufacturers are replacing POP-related chemical compounds with other less-damaging compounds.

Creative Chemists

If you are curious and imaginative, and if you like to figure out how to make and do new things, you might enjoy a career as a chemist.

Chemists at Work

Chemists work in many different environments. Analytic chemists study the components, or parts, of different substances in order to understand their properties. Applied chemists put these observations and theories into practical use.

Chemists work in the energy industry to improve the processes of oil refining or to research alternative energy sources, such as **biofuels**. In the medical field, chemists help develop new medicines and materials that doctors can use to heal their patients. The government employs chemists to determine safety regulations for the everyday uses of chemical products. Many chemists conduct their own research but are also teachers, sharing their knowledge with curious students. Everywhere you look, you will see the work of creative chemists.

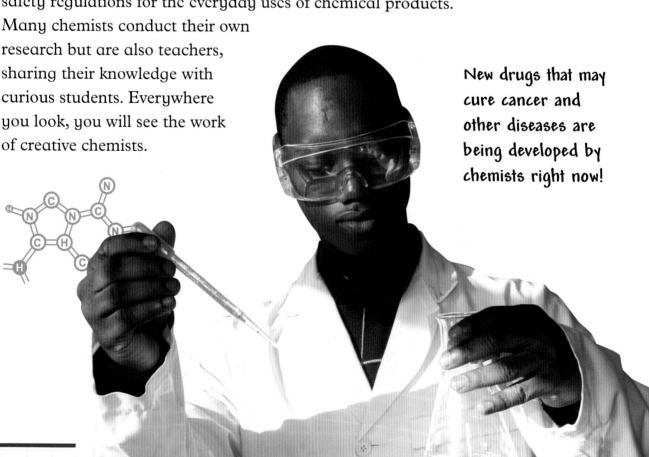

New drugs that may cure cancer and other diseases are being developed by chemists right now!

From Beetles to Buttons

Wherever you are right now, try to count the number of items that are made of plastic. There are probably a lot more than you would have guessed. Would you believe that you have a Southeast Asian beetle to thank for all the plastics you use? Like so many inventions and discoveries, plastic was also discovered through **serendipity** and hard work. Leo Hendrik Baekeland, a chemist, was trying to find an alternative to shellac, which was **excreted** by these beetles and was very expensive to collect. Baekeland made bakelite, the world's first plastic in the early 1900s, from two other substances. Today, most plastics are petroleum products.

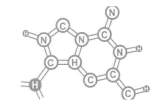

Old phones and radios were made from bakelite, the world's first plastic. Today, plastic is used for everything from toys to toothbrushes, and it is all a result of chemistry.

Want to Learn More?

Whatever the size of your home, the chemistry that makes it and everything in it work, is limitless. Some things, like what happens when you heat water, have been common knowledge for centuries, but there are other aspects of chemistry that scientists are still learning about. If you want to join these scientists in their quests to understand the way the world works, take a look at some of these fascinating resources listed here.

Chemistry Websites:

Rader's Chem4Kids!
www.chem4kids.com
This well organized and detailed website combines snazzy diagrams and multiple-choice quizzes that help you become a science brainiac.

BrainPop
www.brainpop.com/science/matterandchemistry/
Find answers to all your chemistry questions! This interactive site makes learning fun with the help of games, videos, and fascinating animations.

The Exploratorium
www.exploratorium.edu/index.html
The Exploratorium in San Francisco is one of the most exciting science museums in the United States. Thanks to their great website, you can explore from your own home. Read about the science of baseball, or see what happens when you push the button that says "Don't Push this Button!"

Try Science
www.tryscience.org/home.html
Learn trivia, find cool experiments to do at home, and watch live video of scientific projects on this kid-central website.

Chemistry Books:

Why Chemistry Matters series. Crabtree Publishing, 2009. This series uses common examples from everyday life to help explain basic chemistry.

Basher Chemistry: Getting a Big Reaction by Simon Basher and Dan Green. Kingfisher, 2010. This is a fun guide to the secrets of chemistry. Easy-to-understand descriptions of matter's states and properties are accompanied by profiles of important chemists. You will love the drawings that help explain these crazy concepts.

Lucky Science: Accidental Discoveries From Gravity to Velcro, with Experiments by Royston M. Roberts and Jeanie Roberts. Wiley, 1994. Find out more about the role that serendipity plays in science with these fun stories about invention and discovery. You will also find experiments if you want to test some of these revelations out yourself.

Step into Science series. Crabtree Publishing, 2010. Each book in this series explores a step in the scientific method.

Chemistry by Ann Newmark. DK Eyewitness Books, 2005. Did you know that the thread of a spider web is stronger than steel? Or that baking soda can ease the sting of a bee, while vinegar is needed to treat a wasp sting? Learn fascinating trivia and be an eyewitness to the chemical reactions that happen every day with this illustrated reference book.

Places to Learn More:

Chemical Heritage Foundation
Philadelphia, Pennsylvania

The Chemical Heritage Foundation is an organization devoted to sharing the history of and importance of chemistry through exhibits, events, and education. Check out its website at: www.chemheritage.org

National Museum of Natural History
Washington, DC

One of the greatest museums in the world, visitors are free to explore many different exhibits to science, technology, and natural history houses in the various halls of this large museum complex.

Glossary

bacteria Tiny life-forms that can sometimes cause disease

biofuels Any fuel that comes from a renewable biological resource

biologist A person who studies the science of living organisms

carbohydrates Compounds in foods that are broken down by the body for energy

carbon An element that forms the basis for all living things

catalyst A substance that changes the rate of a chemical reaction, but is unchanged chemically

compound Composed of two or more parts, elements, or ingredients

contaminate To make impure

displacement The weight or volume of a liquid that is displaced by an object submerged in it

elements Substances that form the primary parts of matter

enzyme A substance that is produced in living things which produces biochemical reactions

evaporates When the temperature of a liquid increases and it changed into a gas

excreted A substance that is discharged from a plant or animal

filtration When liquid passes through a filter and becomes more pure

impurities Something that makes something else impure or unuseable

influenza virus The virus that causes the flu

matter Everything that occupies space and has mass

mold spores Seeds released by molds or fungal growth that can trigger allergic reactions

pliable Something that can easily bend without cracking or breaking

prism An object that separates the light passing through it into different colors

radar Radio waves used to find speed, direction, and distance of other objects

react To undergo a chemical reaction

salivating To produce saliva, often as a result of seeing or smelling food

serendipity A chance occurrence or happy accident

substance Physical matter or material

Index